George Sidney Guild

Lebanon branch of the Guild family in Connecticut, and some of its descendants:

Supplemental to a genealogy published by L.A. & T. Guild in 1877

George Sidney Guild

Lebanon branch of the Guild family in Connecticut, and some of its descendants:
Supplemental to a genealogy published by L.A. & T. Guild in 1877

ISBN/EAN: 9783337727789

Printed in Europe, USA, Canada, Australia, Japan

Cover: Foto ©ninafisch / pixelio.de

More available books at **www.hansebooks.com**

LEBANON BRANCH

OF THE

GUILD FAMILY

IN

CONNECTICUT,

AND SOME OF ITS

DESCENDANTS.

———◦◇◦———

SUPPLEMENTAL TO A GENEALOGY PUBLISHED
BY L. A. & T. GUILD IN 1877.

By L. A. and G. S. GUILD.

WOODBURY, CONN.:
PRESS OF W. W. WISEGARVER.
1886.

LEBANON BRANCH

—OF THE—

GUILD FAMILY

—IN—

CONNECTICUT

AND SOME OF ITS

DESCENDANTS

Supplemental to a Genealogy Pub.
by L. A. & T. Guild in 1877

BY L. A. & C. S. GUILD

PREFACE.

The object in publishing this pamphlet is to present to those interested the fact, that in the will of Samuel Guild of Lebanon, Conn., dated Feb. 6, 1748-9, we have a record which proves conclusively, that we, and all the descendants of Jeremiah Guild of the fifth generation, can trace our genealogy back to John Guild, who settled in Dedham, Mass., about the year 1636, and the generations in this book are numbered from him. Since the publication of L. A. and T. Guild's book of genealogy, in 1877, it has been found by the records at Lebanon, that Jeremiah Guild, of the fourth generation, married for his first wife Mary Dudley, and had one child, Cynthia; and, that she was a half sister of Mary, Samuel and Jeremiah Guild, (born at Middletown), children of Jeremiah and Elinor (Evarts) Guild, is fully proved by the will of their grandfather mentioned above, and published herein. And we publish some additional records of descendants of Samuel Guild of Lebanon, which have recently been collected from different sources; and also some records, found in Lebanon, of the family of Israel Guild, born in Dedham, 1690, who was a brother of the above-named Samuel.

L. A. AND G. S. GUILD.

Bethlehem, Conn., June 2, 1886.

THE NATIONALITY OF THE "GUILD" FAMILY.

N a letter written by Calvin Guild, Dedham, Mass., Oct.
22, 1857, to Truman Guild, Milton, Conn., he says:
"Dear Sir: Your esteemed favor of the 10th inst. is received, for which please accept my thanks. You say that
probably your grandfather originated in Guilford, Conn., and
that his ancestors were natives of Wales. In the latter part of
your conjecture I think you are mistaken. I have conversed
with Benj. Guild, Esq., a lawyer in Boston, now 84 years old,
who has been in England and Scotland, who took much pains
to ascertain the truth of the tradition you speak of. He says
he learned beyond a doubt that our ancestors were natives of
Scotland. He also obtained an impress of the old coat of arms
of the "Guild family," (there pronounced "Gild," the "u"
silent), and now carries it as a watch seal. I think I can give
the genealogy of your ancestors; at least I hope so, for I am
desirous of finding that John Guild who came to this
country about the year 1630, and first settled in Watertown,
Mass., and then colonized with a few others from that town
in Dedham in 1636, is the common ancestor of all of the name
in New England. He married Elizabeth Crooke, in 1645, and
had seven children, two only of whom I have been able to find
any descendants for, viz; Samuel and John. ²Samuel was born
Sept. 7, 1647, and Sept. 29, 1676, he married Mary Wood-
cock, and had 10 children; of these ³Samuel was born Oct. 12,
1677; Jan. 8, 1700, he married Sarah Hartshorn and had five

children, viz: ⁴Sarah, born Dec. 26, 1702, ⁴Samuel, born Sept.
27, 1704, ⁴Mary, born July 25, 1707, ⁴Jeremiah, born July 3,
1711, and ⁴Phebe, born April 26, 1713. Thus far I find the
records in our town book trace their children no farther. Now
I hope to find that you are of the lost tribe of Jeremiah. There
is another family of the name in Connecticut that I hope to
trace to the same source. Yours Very Truly, C. GUILD, JR."

In another letter of a later date Mr. C. Guild writes:

DEDHAM, MASS., Aug. 24, 1877.

DEAR SIR: I have received from our postmaster a letter
from you, dated 22d, to which I am very glad to reply, for I
am interested to get the name and place or home of any Guild
in this wide world. I send you by mail a copy of my book,
the "Guild Family." As you will find in my preface, two
brothers came to Dedham, viz: John and Samuel. John re-
mained here, and from him sprang all the Guilds named in
my book. I shall be very glad to have your family records
collected and the connection made with mine. You will per-
ceive that a considerable number of names are found prevail-
ing in each branch, which makes it more certain to me that
the families are connected. Any further communication from
you will be gladly received. Yours Very Truly,

To Lewis H. Guild, Esq., Amenia, N. Y.   CALVIN GUILD.

In researches for records of the Guild family, (by George S.
Guild), since a genealogy was published by L. A. & T. Guild
in 1877, some records were found in Windham, Lebanon and So.
Coventry, Ct., wherein one Samuel Guild, of the 3d generation,
between the years April 1713 and October 1716, moved from
Dedham, Mass., with his family to Windham, Conn., where
his seventh child ⁴Elizabeth was born Oct. 6, 1716. In the records taken from Lebanon is a deed of land to Samuel Guild,
of Windham, from Joseph Swetland, dated July 22, 1717; also, ⁴Abigail Guild, daughter of Samuel and Sarah Guild, was
born June 19, 1721. (In the Lebanon records is recorded the

births of children and grandchildren of this Samuel Guild's brother, Israel, as appears further on.)

4th gen.—Samuel Guild, jun., and Katherine Allen were married together Sept 15, 1731. [He was born at Dedham, Mass., Sept 27, 1704, and died March 6, 1771, of small pox, and, with two others, was buried in a field near the house of Giles Little, in Columbia, Conn. Three large tombstones once marked the place, but have been removed to the corner of the fence by the roadside.] Children, Phebe, b. June 5, 1732, Temperance, b. Dec. 15, 1733, Jabez, b. Aug. 20, 1735, died Aug. 7, 1742, Lois, b. June 26, 1745, Samuel, b. Nov. 11, 1749, d. July 29, 1831.

5th gen.—Phebe Guild married Stephen Hunt, jun., April 3, 1755; child, Sibyl, b. May 13, 1757.

5th gen.—Temperance Guild married Joseph Hibbert. Aug. 7, 1755.

4th gen.—Sarah Guild married Dea. James Wright, Apr. 23, 1724; children, Susanna, b. Aug. 21, 1725, James, b. Mar, 21, 1727, Jabez, b. Apr. 24, 1728, Sarah, b. Feb. 15, 1731, Irene, b. Feb. 4, 1733, John, b. Feb. 20, 1736, Joseph, b. July 4, 1738, Jeriah, b. Sept. 26, 1741.

4th gen.—Mary Guild married Dea. Thomas Lyman Jan. 25, 1727; children, Mary, b. Feb. 20, 1728, Sarah, b. June 11, 1730, Eunice, b. July 29, 1732, Rachel, b. Apr. 15, 1735, Thomas, b. June 28, 1737, Mary, b. May 19, 1739, Hannah, b. Aug. 4, 1741, Joseph and Benjamin, twins, b. July 6, 1744, Daniel, b. July 9, 1746, Rachel, b. Sept. 3, 1747, Abigail, b. May 5, 1752.

4th gen.—Jeremiah Guild m. 1st, Mary Dudley, Nov. 11, 1731; child, Cynthia, b. Sept. 15, 1732.

5th gen.—Cynthia Guild married John Woodward Sept. 7, 1752; children, Nehemiah, b. Aug. 14, 1753, Triphena, b. Dec. 4, 1754.

4th gen —Phebe Guild married Samuel Woodward Jan. 24,

1732; children, Phebe, b. Oct. 30, 1733, Samuel, b. Nov. 5, 1735, Rhoda, b. Feb. 8, 1738.

4th gen.—Elizabeth Guild married John Sweatland, jun., Apr. 15, 1736; children, Elizabeth, b. May 6, 1737, John, b. Apr. 12, 1739, Cynthia, b. June 24, 1742, Samuel, b. Aug. 21, 1744.

4th gen.—Abigail Guild married Benjamin Abel.

————O————

THE WILL OF SAMUEL GUILD, OF THE 3D GEN.

————

In the name of God, amen. The 6th day of February, 1748–9, I, Samuel Guild, of Lebanon, in the county of Windham, Connecticut Colony. in New England, being sick and weak in body, but of sound mind and memory, thanks be given to God: therefore calling unto mind the mortality of my body, and knowing that it is appointed for all men once to die, do make and ordain this my last Will and Testament: That is to say, principally and first of all, I give and recommend my soul into the hands of God that gave it, and my body I recommend to the earth to be buried in decent Christian burial, at the discretion of my executors. nothing doubting but at the general resurrection I shall receive the same again by the mighty power of God: and as touching such earthly estate wherewith it has pleased God to bless me in this life, I give, devise and dispose of the same in the following manner and form:

Imprimis.—I give and bequeath to Sarah, my dearly beloved wife, the sum of twenty-five pounds in bills of publick credit, of the old tenor, making good to her the discount or sink of s'd

bills of credit to be levied out of my estate, together with all my household goods, debts, and movable effects, and likewise my dwelling-house, that is to say that part of it which I built, exclusive from the other part which my son Samuel built for himself, to be improved by her during her natural life: and furthermore, so much cyder and appels out of my part of the orchard as shall be needful for her support during her natural life. Likewise to be allowed a sufficiency of fire-wood.

Item.—I give to my well beloved son Samuel Guild, my cane with which I used to walk, or in lieu thereof twenty shillings of ye tenor

Item.—I give to the heirs of my well beloved son Jeremiah Guild, deceased: in the first place I give to my well beloved granddaughter, Cynthia Guild, daughter of ye above sd Jeremiah Guild, the sum of five pounds, old tenor.

Item.—I give Mary Guild, daughter of said Jeremiah Guild, the sum of five pounds, old tenor.

Item.—I give Samuel Guild, son to the above sd Jeremiah Guild, the sum of five pounds in bills of credit of the old tenor.

Item.—I give to my grandson, Jeremiah Guild, son to said Jeremiah Guild, deceased, the sum of five pounds in bills of publick credit of the old tenor.

Item.—I likewise give all the remainder of my estate which I have not already given and disposed of, in this my last will and testament, to my five daughters: that is to say, to my well beloved daughter Sarah, the wife of James Wright; to my well beloved daughter Mary, the wife of Thomas Lyman; to Phebe my well beloved daughter, the wife of Samuel Woodward; to my well beloved daughter Elizabeth, the wife of John Sweatland; to my well beloved daughter Abigal, the wife of Benjamin Abel; which estate hereby given to these my daughters, here above named, shall be equally divided between them, each one having an equal proportion. Again, I likewise constitute, make and ordain my trusty and well beloved sons-in-

law, James Wright and Samuel Woodward, to be my executors of this my last will and testament: and I do hereby disannul, revoke and disallow all and every other former wills, testaments, legacy and bequests executed by me, in any ways before named, willed and bequeathed, ratifying and confirming this and no other to be my last will and testament. In witness whereof I have hereunto set my hand and seal the day and year above written.

SAMUEL GUILD. { SEAL. }

Signed, sealed, published, pronounced and declared by the said Samuel Guild as his last will and testament, in the presence of us the subscribers.   JACOB SPOFORD.
                                             ROBERT BENNETT.
June 23d, 1750.   WM. LINES.

Then Jacob Spoford and Robert Bennett, both of them personally known to me, appeared before me, the subscriber, and made solemn oath that they saw the within named Samuel Guild, the testator, sign, seal, publish, pronounce and declare the within written to be his last will and testament, and that they signed as witnesses in his presence, and that they saw William Lines sign as a witness, at the same time, and they judged the testator to be of sound mind and memory at the same time.   JOSEPH CLARK, JUSTICE OF THE PEACE.

At a Court of Probate held at Lebanon, in the district of Windham, June 25, 1750, Jonathan Trumbull, Judge.

Then the last will and testament of Samuel Guild, deceased, was exhibited unto this Court by the executors within mentioned, who accepted that trust in said Court, and took the oath accordingly, the witnesses to said will being sworn, which will is by this Court proved, approved, allowed of and ordered to be recorded and kept on file.

Test, ICHABOD ROBINSON, CLERK OF PROBATE.

12th August, 1751. Then the foregoing will was recorded.
                              ICHABOD ROBINSON, Clerk Probate.

WILL OF SARAH GUILD.

The following will of Sarah Guild has been found in the Windham Probate Records, book 4, page 118:

Will of Sarah Guild, relict of Samuel, of Lebanon, dec'd. In the name of God, amen. The 6th of July, 1750, I, Sarah Guild, of Lebanon, in County of Windham, widow and relict to Mr. Samuel Guild, of Lebanon, dec'd, &c.

Imprimis.—I give to my son Samuel Guild my gun given to me by my husband.

Item.—I give to my grandson, Samuel Guild, eldest son to my son Jeremiah Guild, dec'd, £1.

Item.—I give unto my grandson, Jeremiah Guild, £1.

"   "   "   granddaughter, Cynthia Guild, £1.

"   "   "   "   Mary   "   £1.

Item.—I give unto my beloved daughters, Sarah Wright, Mary Lyman, Phœbe Woodward, Elizabeth Sweatland, and Abigail Abel, all my personal property given to me by last will and testament of my husband, share and share alike.

And I make and constitute my son-in-law, Thomas Lyman, my executor.

Witnesses,
JACOB SPOFFORD,
ISRAEL THORS,
ROBERT BENNETT.

her
SARAH X GUILD. { SEAL. }
mark.

---o---

The following record is from L. A. and T. Guild's book, and from records at Middletown, Conn.:

Fourth Generation.—Jeremiah Guild married (second wife)

Elinor Evarts, daughter of James and Mary (Carter) Evarts. She was born in East Guilford, (now Madison), Dec. 9, 1711. Mary Evarts deeded land to Elinor Guild in Middletown, Conn., Feb. 25, 1744. Children,

Mary ———, m. ——— Marshall; resided somewhere in the State of New York; Samuel, b. Jan. 3, 1743, died in 1815; Jeremiah, b. Sept. 4, 1746. d. Jan. 31, 1822.

5th gen.—Samuel Guild married Abigail Doolittle, Jan. 28, 1762. Children, Mary, b. Nov. 22, 1762, Artimesey, b. Dec. 22, 1764, Phelix, b. Oct 1, 1766, Cynthia, b. Nov. 3, 1768, Jeremiah, b. Nov. 3, 1770, Elinor Evarts, b. Sept. 19, 1772, Plural, b. Apr. 23, 1775, died Feb. 23, 1776.

5th gen.—Jeremiah Guild, m. Hannah Hale; b. June 27, 1756, d. May. 9, 1800, in Warren, Conn.; m. for his second wife, Sept. 1800, Lucinda Fenton, b. Nov. 13, 1768, d. Feb. 22; 1849.

Children by first wife: Sally b. July 16, 1777, d. July 13, 1810, Timothy, b. Oct. 21, 1779, d. Dec. 25, 1838, Gad, b. Mar. 31, 1782, d. May 16, 1860, Alban, b. Aug. 21, 1784, d. May 28, 1874, Everitt, b. Apr. 3, 1786, d. Apr. 25, 1850, Desdemona, b. Nov. 4. 1789, d. May 26, 1871, Jeremiah, b. Apr. 15, 1792, d. Aug. 18, 1859, (our father), Clarissa, b. Aug. 3, 1794, d. Aug. —, 1847, Polly, b. Mar. 24, 1797, d. May 20, 1881.

Children by second wife: Lucinda, b. June 16, 1801, d. July 4, 1881, Frederick F., b. Feb. 6, 1803. d. Sept., 1854, Sophronia, b. Oct. 20, 1804, d. March 26, 1870, Truman, b Apr. 19, 1806, Anna M., b. Aug. 6, 1808.

———o———

The following records, not heretofore published, of descend ants of Samuel Guild, (who died in Lebanon, Conn., 1750), were collected by George S Guild, from Mrs. S. P. Loomis,

South Coventry, Conn., Mrs. C. G. Frink, St. Louis, Mo., Mrs. Polly W. Guild, Harford, Pa., and A. W. Boynton, Bridgeport, Conn.

5th gen.—Samuel Guild, (b. Nov. 14, 1749), married Hannah Newcomb. Children. Silas, b. 1776, d. Apr. 21, 1840, Clarissa, b. 1779, d. Feb. 3, 1812, Samuel, b. Oct. 28, 1781, d. Jan. 14, 1847, at Harford, Pa., Lois, b. 1786, d. June 25, 1851.

6th gen.—Silas Guild married, Sept. 1, 1796, Susanna Walker, b. Apr. 12, 1778. Child, Gerry, b. March 25, 1812, d. March 18, 1872, at Pittsfield, Mass.

6th gen.—Clarissa Guild married John Dow, of Coventry, Conn. Children. Diantha, b. 1800, Almira, b. 1802, d. Aug. 5, 1877, John N., b. Feb. 5, 1805, d. Jan. 7, 1865, Silas Newcomb, d. Mar. 23, 1876.

6th gen.—Samuel Guild married Hannah Coleman, b. Dec. 5, 1783, d. Jan. 3, 1871. Children. Sally, b. Dec. 6, 1803, r. Great Bend, Pa.; Rockwell, b. Apr. 2, 1805, d. Oct. 3, 1855, Lois, b. Feb. 10, 1807, d. Sept. 20, 1856, Silas Brewster, b. June 1, 1809, r. Harford, Pa.; Alvira, b. Feb. 1, 1811, d. Mar. 24, 1879, Lysander, b. Mar. 23, 1813, Harlan, b. July 10, 1815, d., Aug. 2, 1836, Temperance, b. Sept. 12, 1817, Hannah, b. July 22, 1821, Susanna, b. July, 15, 1823, r. West Troy, N. Y., Catharine, b. July 21, 1826, d. Oct. 3, 1881.

6th gen.—Lois Guild married Dea. John Boynton, lived and died near Coventry pond, owned a factory, and made carding-machines. Children. John Watson, b. July 22, 1811, at Columbia, Ct, d. 1879; Leander Wolcott, b. Aug. 23, 1813, at Columbia, Almanzor Winslow, b. Sept. 21, 1815, at Coventry; Conn.

7th gen.—Gerry Guilds married Jane Homer, of Boston, Mass. Children, Caroline Gardiner, b. Oct. 6, 1835, Mary Jane, b. June 18, 1838, Sarah Frances, b. Sept. 15, 1840, George Gerry, b. March 27, 1846, d. March 16, 1847, Frank

Gerry, b. July 21, 1851. *Caroline G. Guilds m. Seth Frink, Sept. 6, 1854. *Mary J. Guilds m. Harvey Russell, Apr. 25, 1858. Child, George. *Sarah F. Guilds m. Henry W. Holden, May 25, 1859. *Frank G. Guilds m. Alice Phillips, Sept. 10, 1873. Child, George.

7th gen.—Diantha Dow married Soloman P. Loomis, of South Coventry, Ct.

7th gen.—Almira Dow married Samuel Wilson. Children, John D., Catharine, Lorenzo Dow.

7th gen.—John N. Dow married Mary Porter. Children, Lorenzo F., b. May 26, 1841, d. Sept. 1, 1873, Arthur. b. Feb. 19, 1815.

7th gen.—Sally Guild married Amasa Chase. Child, Simeon Brewster, b. Apr. 18, 1827, m. May 1, 1851, Fannie DuBois. Resides at Great Bend, Pa.

7th gen.—Rockwell Guild married Mary Thatcher. Children, Jane E., b. Jan 6, 1828, m. John A. Thatcher, r. Downer's Grove, Ill.; Adelia Betsey, b. Nov. 7, 1829, d. Apr. 20, 1886, m. John Jassoy, d. Nov. 21, 1876; Nancy C., b. July 17, 1834, m. John Staudt. r. Aurora. Ill.; Hannah C., b. Aug. 11, 1837, d. Aug. 6, 1855, Samuel F., b. Oct. 5, 1840, d. Oct. 7, 1841, Harlan B., b. Aug. 12, 1843, d. Dec. 15, 1843, Ellen M., b. July 7, 1846, d. Sept. 11, 1870, m. Noah E. Gary.

7th gen.—Lois Guild married Simeon Tucker. Children, Amanda F., b. Mar., 1827, m. Theodore Gamble, Amasa B., b. Sept. 1829, m. Elizabeth Gamble, d. Feb., 1885; 2d wife, Emma P. Gamble; r. Aurora, Ill. *Susanna, b. Dec., 1831, m. William Williams, d. in the war. Child, Mortimer K., m. Mar. 17, 1885, Elizabeth Harding, d. 1886; Louisa, b. Aug., 1834, m. Peter Couran, r. Kansas.

7th gen.—Silas Brewster Guild married Catharine Chase, d. Children, Melissa J., b. Oct. 14, 1831, Sarah, C. b. July 28, 1834, d. Jan. 27, 1879, Winslow Boynton, b. Apr. 5, 1841.

S. B. Guild married second wife Polly W. Tyler.   ⁵Melissa J. Guild m. March 19, 1856, J. N. Wilson, M. D., dead.   Children, Edgar A., b. Feb. 33, 1857, d. Aug. 8. 1858, Arthur J., b. Jan. 8, 1860, Charlie R., b. Feb. 1. 1868.   ⁵Sarah C. Guild m. Nov. 7, 1852, Charles H. Miller.   Children, Catharine, b. July 28, 1853, d. Aug. 28, 1859, Edward W., b. Dec. 1, 1855, Nellie, b. Feb. 1, 1858, d. Aug. 18, 1859, Fannie J., b. Dec. 14, 1861, d. May 8, 1879. ⁹Edward W. Miller m. Feb. 26, 1878, Mary E. Osborn.   Children, Roy Winslow, b. Oct. 21, 1878, Harry Edward, b. Sept. 15, 1879, Mabel Fanny, b. Nov. 9, 1880, Fred O., b. Dec. 6, 1881, Eddie, b. Jan. 6, 1883, Maud May, b. March, 1884.   ⁵Winslow B. Guild m. Oct. 15, 1861, H. Amelia Edwards.   Child, Jennie Louisa, b. May 8, 1863. m. Dec. 18, 1884, D. A. Capewell, M. D.

7th gen.—Alvira Guild married Abel Read. jun.   Children, Adeline m. Edward Sheppard, r. Brooklyn. N. Y.; Wellington m. Helen Burrows, Ann m. Henry C. Moxley, Eleanor m. Rev. Stephen Elwell, Everitt m. Candace Green.

7th gen.—Lysander Guild m. Abigail Moss, Children, Ellen, Cornelia.   **2017926**

7th gen.—Temperance Guild m. John Blanding, died Aug. 5, 1882.   Children, Harlan G., b. May 23, 1837, m. Elizabeth Sibley, resides at Binghampton, N. Y.; Emma Gertrude, b. July 13, 1844, married, Oct. 10, 1883, Sylvester S. Carpenter, M. D.; Mary M., b. June 12, 1854, married Charles Underwood.

7th gen.—Hannah Guild m. Obed G. Coughlan.   Children, Julia A., b. June 30, 1838, Mary D., Merritt, Evans, d., Samuel. ⁵Julia A. Coughlan m. Henry Judson Tyler, d.   Child, Mary E., b. Aug. 5. 1862, m. Jan. 16, 1884, W. W. Fletcher, M. D.   Julia A. Tyler married second husband, Henry Estabrook.

7th gen. —Susanna Guild married. Sept. 12, 1847, Stephen W. Breed, d. Dec. 29, 1880.   Child, Rev. George Breed, r. West Troy, N. Y.

7th gen.—Catharine Guild m. George M. Gamble.   Children, John K., b. Apr. 24, 1850, m. Jennie Tanner Aug. 5. 1882; Ida, Lela, Porter, d., killed with a gun.

7th gen.—John W. Boynton m., May 2, 1832, Eunice Stanley, b. May 26, 1811, at Cairo, N. Y.   Children, born at Coventry, Conn., Mary, b. April 3, 1833, John Everill, b. May 24, 1834, d. 1852, James Henry, b. June 19, 1836, Edward Stanley, b. July 22, 1838, Eliza, b. Feb. 28, 1840, d. 1865, Arthur, b. Sept. 5, 1842, Alice, b. Nov. 7, 1845, Grace Stanley, b. May 3, 1848, Eunice Stanley, b. March 3. 1850. J. W. Boynton m. Caroline Reynolds of E. Hartford, Ct., for second wife.

7th gen.—Leander W. Boynton m. Mary A. Fuller, of Hampton, Conn.   Child, Wolcott Fuller, b. Coventry, Conn.

7th gen.—Almanzor W. Boynton m., Sept. 1, 1846, Harriet Curtis, of Coventry, d. 1856.   Children, LAmour A., b. Dec. 5, 1847, Lillian, b. Feb. 5, 1849, d. 1857.

There are records at Lebanon, Conn., of the births of children and grandchildren of Israel Guild, a brother of Samuel of the 3d generation, as follows:

3d gen.—Israel and Sarah Guild, their children, Deborah, b. June 26, 1715. Hannah, b. Feb. 14, 1717, Keziah. b. May 26, 1719, Jacob, b. Aug. 1, 1722, Israel, b. Nov. 25, 1729, Sarah, b. Dec. 5, 1732.

4th gen.—Deborah Guild m. John House. Sept. 6, 1739. Children, Sarah, b. June 2, 1740. Deborah, b. Apr. 6, 1742, John, b. Apr. 29, 1744. Elijah. b. Sept. 27, 1745, Meny, b. Oct.9, 1747, Phebe, b. June 26, 1749, Simon, b. Mar. 2, 1751.

4th gen.—Jacob Guild married Widow Hannah Larrabee, of Coventry, May 26, 1757.   Children, Levina, b. Mar. 11, 1758, Joseph, b. July 23, 1760.

4th gen.—Sarah Guild m. William Frazer, of Norwich, June 23, 1760.   Children, James Pettis, b. May 28, 1761, John. b. March 18, 1765.

Mr. Spencer Guild, of Milford, N. H., in a letter to Mr.
Calvin Guild, of Dedham, Mass.:

MILFORD, N. H., Oct. 6, 1857.

CALVIN GUILD, JR., ESQ.:

DEAR SIR:—Yours in regard to the Guild family came duly
to hand, and I am sorry to be under the necessity of neglect-
ing to answer so long, and hope what I have to communicate
may still be in season, if of any importance. As regards
Guilds in this State I know nothing, save by report. There
was a family that lived in Francestown some years since, (so I
am informed), but before I came here, and I know nothing of
their history. I think there are none there now. I came from
Vermont to this place and located some 5 years ago. My
brother Asa came one year later, and we and our small families are the only persons I know of by the name of Guild in
the State. I will now give the history in brief of my progen-
itors as far back as I can trace them. My great grandfather's
name was Jacob, and had his origin and I think lived in early
life in Lebanon, Conn., what was then known as Lebanon
Crank. He moved to Hatfield, Mass., and settled on the Connecticut River, in a neighborhood known as West Farms. He
had five sons and two daughters, Joseph, Jesse, Nathaniel, Silas, Israel, Lavinia and Hannah. Joseph and Jesse married
sisters by the name of Smith. Joseph had no children. Jesse was my grandfather. Both served in the war of the Revolution, underwent great privations, and were slightly rewarded
by Joseph's being promoted to, and received a, captain's com-
mission, and Jesse was made orderly sergeant. Joseph finally
returned to Hatfield, where he ever afterwards lived, and died
a few years since at an advanced age. Jesse married early, I
think at the age of 19, (having served three years previous in
the war), and removed to Halifax, Vt., where he followed the
trade of blacksmith, and at the same time tilled the soil. He
lived to the age or 84, and died only some ten years since. He

had five sons and two daughters, Chester, Calvin, Israel, Asa, Hannah, Joel and Elizabeth. Chester had a family, but no sons that lived to grow up. He lived and died in Halifax; his family are now there. Calvin is my father and now lives in Halifax, Vt., on the same farm where he was born, and where my grandfather ever lived after he went to Vermont My father has a family of 8 children. Their names are as follows: William, Asa, Spencer, Julia, Sarah G., Phineas R., Thomas W., Rufus B. My oldest brother William lives on the farm with father. Asa is in this place in a store, and I am also engaged in trade. Julia married Luke Kingsbury, and has recently removed to Wayne, Ill. Sarah married her cousin Albert Guild, son of Israel Guild. The others are unmarried. Phineas R. is a physician in Plainfield, Ill.; Thomas W. is a cutter in a clothing store in Boston, Mass.; Rufus B. is in Knox College, Galesburg, Ill. Israel (son of Jesse) had a family of four sons and two daughters. Their names were Eunice, Lyman, William, Albert, Harriet and Cornelius. All are living except Lyman, who died some three or four years since. All are settled in Wayne, Ill. I know very little of them save Albert, who married my sister Sarah, and is a very thrifty merchant. The others are reported thrifty farmers. Joel moved to Pennsylvania when young or soon after, married and died there, leaving a family of which I know nothing. Cannot now give the names excepting one whose name is Jesse. Asa enlisted in the war of 1812, and never returned. Hannah and Elizabeth were neither married. Hannah died in 1836. Elizabeth is still living in Halifax.—Now to return to my grandfather's brothers, younger than himself: Israel married and had a family, and after his sons were grown up all moved West, to what place I cannot now tell. Their names, so far as I can now recall them, were Joseph, George, Dyer, and some daughters whose names I have forgotten. His son Joseph now lives in Buffalo, N. Y. Nathaniel married and mov-

ed to Hartford, Vt., where he died in middle life. I know nothing of his family, though I think some of them are now living there. Silas, I know nothing of his history save he was somewhat roving in his disposition. I cannot tell whether he is now living or not. Lavinia married a man by the name of Snow and lived in Whately, Mass; she died in early life, or I think before the meridian. Hannah married a man by name of Parker and settled in the easterly part of Whately; she died last year, being over 90 years of age. She and my grandfather both retain their physical and mental capacities in a remarkable degree till late in life; the others I did not know so well in their later years. The family or race of Guilds to which I belong are usually physically tall, straight, slim, rather long, rather thin, marked features, high foreheads, have great firmness, and usually tenacious of an opinion. Perhaps you will be able to form an opinion from names, origin and general physiological character whether we are " kin " or not.

Yours Truly,

SPENCER GUILD.

LOCKPORT, N. Y., Feb. 24, 1880.

MR. L. A. GUILD:

DEAR SIR:—My grandfather's name was Joel Guild, my father's, John Guild, my mother's name, before marriage, Miriam Hoyt. Father and mother came from Vermont, but whether they were born there or not I could not say. We came to Lockport, N. Y., in 1817, a short time after my father's death, and have resided here since. My mother died some four years since, or I could give you particulars more definite. My father done a dry goods business in Utica, N. Y., 'up to the time of his death. Since I come to think of it, I think his father, Joel, lived only a few miles out of Utica, as I have heard mother say he used to drive in. Yours Respectfully,

C. S. GUILD.

RUPERT, VT., Dec. 17, 1877.

MR. L. A. GUILD:

DEAR SIR:—My grandfather's name was John Guild. He came, I think, from Attleboro, Mass. He served 3 months in the Revolution, afterwards went to manufacturing buttons, combs, etc.; moved from there to Lansingburgh, N. Y., and from there to Powlet, Vt., where he died at the age of 85, some 30 years ago. He had three sons, Chauncey, Milton and Pliny, three daughters, Eunice, Lucy and Abigal. Chauncey was my father; he died a few years since aged 80. I had three brothers and four sisters, all living now but one, Walter. My great-grandfather's name I do not know, but will find out shortly, as he has one daughter yet living. Yours Truly,

J. H. GUILD.

RUPERT, VT., Jan. 15, 1878.

MR. L. A. GUILD:

I have found my grandfather's old Bible, and will give you all I can learn from it. My grandfather, John Guild, was born July 28, 1763; married Margaret Doggett May, 1788. His father's name I have not learned. His brothers and sisters were born in the following order: Hannah, Napthali, Eunice, Lucy, John, Abigal. The Bible does not tell where he was born or married. Yours Truly,   J. H. GUILD.